. . . and these thy gifts

Gift of LOVE

by
Thomas Brown
Aileen Giannelli

Elizabeth McMahon Jeep
Revision Editor

OUR SUNDAY VISITOR, INC.
Huntington, Indiana

Project Editor
Margaret Savitskas

Consultants
Edward J. Murray
Nancy Smyczynski Stolfe

Nihil Obstat: Rev. John Kuzmich
Censor Librorum

Imprimatur: William McManus, D.D.
Bishop of Fort Wayne-South Bend
April 19, 1983

ISBN 0-87973-028-5

Published, printed, and bound in the United States of America by
Our Sunday Visitor, Inc.
200 Noll Plaza
Huntington, Indiana 46750

028

ACKNOWLEDGMENTS

Scripture texts used in this work are taken from the New American Bible, © 1970, and the Lectionary for Mass, © 1970 by the Confraternity of Christian Doctrine, Washington, D.C., and are used by license of said copyright owner. No part of the New American Bible may be reproduced in any form without permission in writing from the copyright owner. All rights reserved.

Excerpts from the English translation of the Order of Mass © 1969 by the International Committee on English in the Liturgy, Inc. All rights reserved.

Cover Design by Marcella Keller
Book design, art, and mechanicals by John D. Firestone & Associates, Inc., and James E. McIlrath of Our Sunday Visitor, Inc.

Photo Credits: John D. Firestone & Associates, Inc., pages viii, 1, 2, 5c, 9, 10, 11ab, 13, 18, 22, 24, 25ab, 29, 30, 31, 32, 34b, 35, 45, 51, 52, 62, 66, 69, 74, 76, 78b, 80, 85, 91ad, 92d, 95, 108, 110ac, 111, 117, 119b, 123, 127 (photos designated abc, etc., read left to right); Dr. Tom Dooley's Cause, page 71; all other photos by John Zierten and Diane Garnette of Our Sunday Visitor, Inc.

Contents

Unit 3   Jesus Is Our Savior

Unit 4   Jesus Is Our Leader

Unit 5 God Feeds His People

Unit 6 We Give Thanks Through Jesus

Dear Second Graders,

Gifts are great! We give gifts to those we love. They give gifts to us. Do you remember the last time you received a gift? Who gave it to you? Did you receive it on a special day? Or did you receive it just because someone loved you?

God has given us many gifts. God gives us these gifts out of love. In this book you will learn about God's greatest gift to us. This gift is Jesus Christ. Jesus loved people. He helped them and healed them. When he returned to his Father, he left seven special gifts, called sacraments. Sacraments keep people close to Jesus. The sacraments are signs of Jesus' love for us. They bring his help into our lives. They bring Jesus to us!

In the sacrament of the Eucharist, Jesus shares his life with us. In the sacrament of penance, Jesus gives us his peace and forgiveness. We hope that this book will help you share your life with others and help you grow in peace and love.

Your friends,

Thomas Brown

Aileen Giannelli

UNIT 1

God Gives Us a Home

I Give and Receive Gifts

CHAPTER 1

Here is a riddle. Do you know the answer?

What can be many shapes, many sizes, many colors?

What has no mouth, but says something?

The answer is — a GIFT!

Tell a story about these gifts.
What do they say?

1

Gifts are given by someone who loves you.

When do you receive gifts? When do you give gifts?

You can make any day special by giving someone a gift.

We Believe:

Every good gift,
every perfect gift,
comes from our Father
whose love can never change.

from James 1.17

We Do:

Before you go to sleep tonight, think of two gifts that God has given you.
Thank God in your heart.

CHAPTER 2

I Belong to a Family

We do not begin life all alone.

We begin in a family.

A family is people.

A family is love.

A family is safety.

A family is home.

A family is happiness.

A family is comfort when times are bad.

People in a family take care of each other.

They help each other. They try to make each other happy.

Families are the best way we have of living together.

Every family has a name. What is your family name?
Saint Paul told us that God is the Father who gives his name
to every family!

from Ephesians 3.14

Look at the pictures. They are all pictures of families.

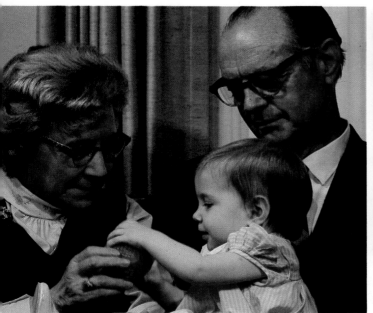

How are these families alike?

Jesus had a family. He had a mother named Mary and a foster father named Joseph. He had a grandmother and a grandfather, a cousin named John, and other relatives, too. Jesus loved his family very much.

Jesus is the Son of God, our Father. He is the brother of ALL people. That makes us one very big family! Jesus loves all of us very much.

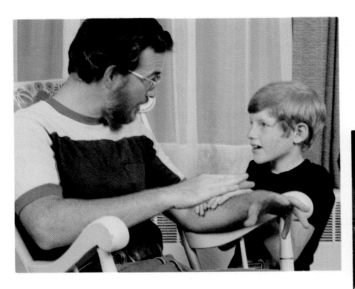

Those who love us are a gift of God, our Father.
When we love and care for each other,
God, our Father, is with us.

7

We Believe:

God, our Father, has given us families because he loves us.
He has given us Jesus as our brother.

We Do:

Pick one member of your family. Do something special for him or her this week. Write your idea on paper so you will not forget.

CHAPTER 3

I Belong to a Neighborhood

Carlos went to the store for his neighbor, Mr. Kelley. He could not reach the rice. Mr. Gomez helped him. "Gracias," said Carlos. "Glad to help you," said Mr. Gomez.

Carlos paid for the food. The bag was big and heavy. When he reached the door, he could not open it. Mrs. King helped him. "Gracias," said Carlos. "Glad to help you," said Mrs. King.

As Carlos walked down the street,
the bag began to tear. Carlos couldn't
carry the bag anymore. His friend
Sylvia helped him. "Gracias," said
Carlos. "Glad to help you," said
Sylvia.

Carlos and Sylvia climbed the stairs
to Mr. Kelley's apartment. Mr.
Kelley was sick and could not leave
his house. "Thanks," said Mr.
Kelley. "Glad to help you," said
Carlos.

Name the good neighbors in this story. How many people helped Carlos?
How many people helped Mr. Kelley?

A friendly neighborhood
is like a strong castle.

from Proverbs 18.19

Good neighbors are a gift from God, our Father.
He gives us neighbors because he loves us.

We Believe:

We should think of our neighbors,
doing good for them
and building up their spirits.

from Romans 15.2

We Do:

All the stars do not live in Hollywood. There are some in your neighborhood.
They make it a good place to live.

Draw a star. Write on it, "YOU ARE A STAR." Give it to one of your good
neighbors.

CHAPTER 4

I Belong to a School Class

All over the world children learn together.

They help each other.

They are kind to each other.

They try to be fair.

They try to give everyone a turn.

Teachers know many things.
They share those things with us.
They help us grow up.
They care about us.

Classmates and teachers are gifts from God, our Father.
He gives us school friends because he loves us.

Jesus listened to the children. What do you think the children said to him?

Jesus loves children. Jesus loves you. Jesus knows you are very important.

Jesus is your teacher.
Jesus is the teacher of your teachers.

15

We Believe:

God said to his people, "Do not forget what I have done for you. Be sure to teach your children all about my love."

from Deuteronomy 4.9

We Do:

Use this prayer to thank God for his love.

I love the Lord because he listens to me;
He bends down to listen
When I talk to him.

I offer thanks to the Lord because he watches over me.
I will walk in his sight
Every day of my life.

The Lord, my God, is very kind.
He cares for little children.
He cares for me.

I will live as the Lord wants me to live.
I will remember his love
Every day of my life.

from Psalm 116

CHAPTER 5

I Belong to a Parish

People who follow Jesus are called Christians. Some Christians are called Catholics.

Catholics work and pray together in parish families. Parish families gather on Sunday to thank God. Parish families try to live as Jesus taught. Members of a parish family try to love and help each other.

Every parish has a name.
What is the name of your parish family?

17

It was Sunday. Claire's mother was sick.
Her father was working. Claire
wanted to go to church, but she had
never gone by herself. Her mother said
that she could go, so Claire went to
church all alone.

When Claire got to church, people were
talking to each other. No one noticed
Claire. No one said "Hello" to her.

Claire felt very alone.

Can you finish this story?

Jesus said, "Where two or three are gathered in my name, I am there with them."

from Matthew 18.20

Jesus is with us when we come together in our parish family.

We Believe:

The people of our parish are gifts to us from God, our Father.
He gives us other Christians because he loves us.

We Do:

Pick one question. Find the answer. Share your answer with the class.
- How do members of your parish family help poor people?
- How do members of your parish learn more about Jesus?
- How do members of your parish teach others about Jesus?

Let's Look Back

A. God shows his love for you through the people he puts in your life. Can you name some people who love you or help you or take care of you? Name one person on each of your ten fingers.

B. Can you tell something about each of these words? You can look in the GLOSSARY on pages 131-133 for help.

Bible	Jesus	Nazareth
Catholic	Joseph	Neighbor
Christian	Mary	Parish

C. Do you remember these stories from the Bible?
Tell one of these stories at home today.

- Joseph and His Family (Genesis 37-47)
- The Woman and Her Coin (Luke 15.8-10)
- Jesus and the Children (Matthew 19.13-15)

Celebration of Belonging

Leader: The Lord be with you.

All: And also with you.

                 . . . .

Leader: What do you ask of God?

All: We want to grow as members of God's family and live forever in his kingdom.

Reader 1:   Father in heaven, we thank you for all those who love us and care for us. We belong to many people and they belong to us. We belong to you, too, Father, and you belong to us. We are ready to praise and thank you.

Reader 2:   A reading from the gospel of Saint John.

All: Glory to you, Lord.

Reader 2:   Jesus said, "As my Father in heaven loves me, so I love you. Live in my love. This is my command: love each other as I have loved you. I choose you to be my friends and I ask you to be friends to one another."

                             from John 15.9-17

                 This is the gospel of the Lord.

All: Praise to you, Lord Jesus Christ.

                 . . . .

Leader: Let us join hands and pray as Jesus taught us.

All: Our Father . . .

UNIT 2

Signs of Love and Growth

Signs Have Secret Meanings

CHAPTER 6

Nancy Hardy, detective, was on another case. Her brother was missing! Where could he be? Look at the clues. Can you help Nancy solve the mystery?

Clues or signs give us a message. What did each of these signs tell Nancy?

Look at these signs. What do they mean? What would you do if you saw them?

Some signs have more than
one meaning. What is the same
in these signs?

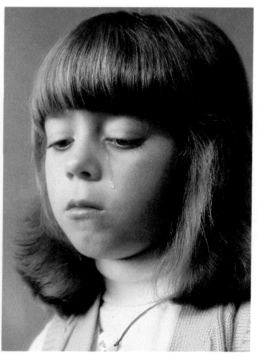

25

We Believe:

We can see God's strength in the things he has made.

from Romans 1.20

We Do:

Look around your neighborhood for signs with secret meanings. Ask a parent or brother or sister for help.

Write down the signs and their meanings.

- Find a sign of God's strength.
- Find a sign of love between people.
- Find a sign of respect between people.
- Find a sign of care for the neighborhood.
- Can you find other signs?

Jesus Is a Sign of Love

CHAPTER 7

Jesus is our way to the Father. He can teach us how to live.
Jesus gave us the Law of Love. He said,
"You shall love the Lord your God,
with all your heart,
with all your soul,
with all your strength,
and with all your mind;
and your neighbor as yourself."

Luke 10.27

Many people listened to Jesus. They
tried to understand. Jesus told them,
"I am the way, and the truth, and
the life. If you really know me, you
will know my Father also."

from John 14.6-7

Many people believed Jesus.
They followed his way.

27

Jesus told a story about a man who found someone hurt on the side of the road. He stopped to help.

Will you help? Will you pass by?

Ana's Lunch

The schoolbell rang for lunch. It was a beautiful day. "You may eat outside today," the teacher said. Many of the children ran to the big tree near their classroom. They sat down. They opened their lunches.

Ana saw Felipe standing far away from the group. She went to him. "What's the matter, Felipe?" she asked. "Where is your lunch?" Felipe said, "My mother is very sick today. I wanted to help her before I left for school. I did not have time to make my lunch." Ana said, "I have a good lunch. Come and share mine."

We Believe:

Those who love God
must also love their brothers and sisters.

from 1 John 4.21

We Do:

Look at the people in your home,
in your school,
and in your neighborhood.
Think about them.
Choose one person to help during this week.

CHAPTER 8

Signs
of Trouble

Henry's car went "Whang! Whang! Whang!" "Now what is the matter?" he said. "My car should go 'Hummmm!' " Henry put his car in the garage. He looked at the motor. Louie and Alice and Carl looked at the motor, too.

"How are you going to fix it?" they asked. "First I have to find the problem," said Henry. "Then I will know what needs to be done." Henry looked at the wires. "No trouble there," he said. He looked at the hose. "No trouble there either." Then Henry saw something. "Look," he said. "The fan blade is bent. The fan was going 'Whang! Whang! Whang!' Now I know how to fix my car."

Henry fixed the fan blade in his car and asked his three friends to come for a ride. When they drove away, Henry's car went "Hummmmmm!"

Sometimes things go Whang! Whang! Whang! inside us. We become worried or unhappy. We want someone to know that we are in trouble. We want someone to help us.

The way you feel can be a sign of trouble.
You must find out what the trouble is.
Then you can fix the problem.

Your parents will help.
Your friends will help.
Your teachers and priests will help.
They love you and want you to be happy.

Zaccheus Meets Jesus

Jesus knew Zaccheus was not happy. People hated him because he took their money. Jesus helped Zaccheus find his problem. "You do not love enough," he said. "You are selfish." Zaccheus told Jesus he was sorry. Zaccheus told his neighbors he was sorry. He gave back the money. Jesus brought Zaccheus peace and happiness.

from Luke 19.1-10

Jesus will bring us peace and happiness.

33

Dan hurt Don by accident.
Everyone has accidents once in a while.
We can have an accident, yet still be
living as Jesus taught us.

Burt hit Bart on purpose.
If we *mean* to hurt someone,
then we are not living as Jesus wants
us to live.

We Believe:

Jesus wants to bring us peace and happiness.

We Do:

When we know something is wrong we can help things become right again.
Remember these four steps:

1. Find the trouble.
2. Fix the trouble.
3. Say you are sorry.
4. Ask for help.

CHAPTER 9

Signs of Life

First we are born.

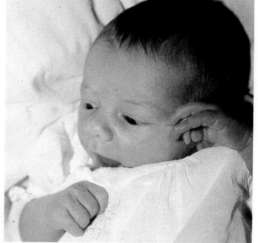

Our bodies grow.
Our minds grow.
We grow, and grow, and grow.

We eat to grow. We eat
to celebrate. We eat
with family and friends.

Growing people need to belong.
When there is trouble we make peace.

We need help when we
are sick. People need
help when they are
dying.

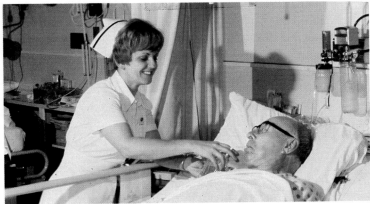

People grow with their families.
People grow with the work they do.
People grow, and grow, and grow.

This is our <u>birth</u> into the Church family.

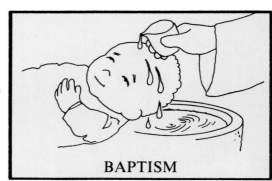

BAPTISM

We need the <u>strength</u> of God to help us grow.

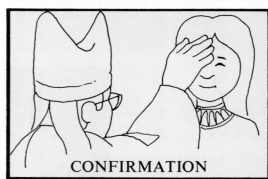

CONFIRMATION

Jesus prepared a holy <u>meal</u> for us.

HOLY EUCHARIST

God forgives us. God helps us make <u>peace</u>.

PENANCE

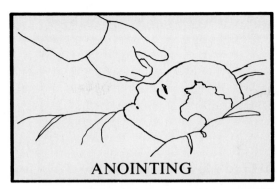

ANOINTING

The Church brings the <u>healing</u> power of Jesus.

MATRIMONY

We can begin a new <u>family</u> of God's people.

HOLY ORDERS

Our Church needs <u>leaders</u>.

These are the sacraments of Jesus and his Church. They are signs of his love for us. They are signs of our life in him.

We Believe:

The seven sacraments are special signs of God's love for us.
Sacraments help the whole Church grow.

We Do:

Can you learn the names of the seven sacraments?
The clue words will help you remember.

BAPTISM   Birth

CONFIRMATION   Strength

HOLY EUCHARIST   Meal

PENANCE   Peace

ANOINTING   Healing

MATRIMONY   Family

HOLY ORDERS   Leaders

Signs of Thanksgiving

CHAPTER 10

God fed the Israelites in the desert.

God fed the Indians. God fed the Pilgrims.

God feeds us.

God asks us to see that none of his children go hungry.

Food is a sign of God's love.

We can thank God for his gift. **41**

We Believe:

The earth's good food is one of the most important signs of God's love for his people. There are many ways to give thanks to God for his good gifts.

We Do:

Use this prayer of thanksgiving.

All: Praise the Lord, my soul!

          O Lord, my God, how great and good you are!

A: You send the rain to make all things sparkle and grow,

          clean water for us to drink.

          O Lord, my God, how great you are!

B: You raise grass on the earth for the cattle,

          and many plants for us to eat.

          O Lord, my God, how great you are!

A: You give wine to make us cheerful, oil to make us healthy,

          and bread to make us strong.

          O Lord, my God, how great you are!

B: Your gifts fill us with joy,

          may you find joy in our prayers of thanksgiving.

          O Lord, my God, how great you are!

All: Praise the Lord, my soul!

          O Lord, my God, how great and good you are!

from Psalm 104

Let's Look Back

A. God made us and he loves us. Can you name some signs of God's strength and love? Name one sign on each of your ten fingers.

B. Can you tell something about each of these words? You can look in the GLOSSARY on pages 131-133 for help.

Anointing	Holy Orders	Penance
Baptism	Law of Love	Sacrament
Confirmation	Matrimony	Thanksgiving
Eucharist		

C. Do you remember these stories from the Bible?
Tell one of these stories at home today.
- The Good Samaritan (Luke 10.25-37)
- Zacchaeus Meets Jesus (Luke 19.1-10)
- Noah and the Rainbow (Genesis 9.8-17)
- The Bread That Came From Heaven (Exodus 16.4-15)

D. Can you explain why we celebrate Thanksgiving Day?

UNIT 3

Jesus Is Our Savior

CHAPTER 11

Jesus Is Our Father's Greatest Gift

God's people love him. They try to follow him. But it is not always easy. Sometimes they act mean and selfish. God wants to help his people.

God the Father sent his Son to be with his people —

— to save them from evil
— to show them the way
— to love and comfort them. **45**

Jesus is the Son of God. Mary, his mother, was the first to know of his coming. She and Elizabeth thanked God for coming to live with his people.

We Believe:

During Advent we thank the Father for sending Jesus to us. We prepare our hearts to celebrate Christmas, the way Mary prepared to welcome Jesus on the day he was born.

We Do:

We light one candle on the Advent wreath. We pray:

1. Come, Lord Jesus; come and save us.

   Show us the glory of God.

   Be our light that shines in the darkness.

   Be our redeemer and protector.

   (Listen to the reading of the Word of God.)

2. O Mary, how holy you are to be the Mother of God.

   O Blessed Mother, we rejoice with you in this holy season of Advent.

3. The Lord is near to all who call on him.

   He himself will come to save us.

   Come, Lord Jesus; come and save us.

   Show us the glory of God. Amen.

CHAPTER 12

Jesus Is Good News

There is a new baby in the Janek family. Everyone is very happy. They will send cards to tell their friends the good news. They will invite their friends to see the new baby.

Jesus is born!
The good news spreads!

An angel told some shepherds,
"Today a savior has been born to you!
This is good news for all the people."
The shepherds hurried to see the child.
They were filled with joy.
The shepherds told their neighbors the good news.
Jesus is born!

from Luke 2.8-18

49

Vol. IXIVIX   No. IIVIXIIYXI   November 30, 1999

JESUS IS HERE!

We Believe:

Jesus Christ, Son of God, Savior of the
World! You are the Lord, you are the
Holy One. You have come to us and
you will never leave us.

We Do:

We light two candles on the
Advent wreath. We pray:

1. Come, Lord Jesus; come and save us.
   Show us the glory of God.
   Be our light that shines in the darkness.
   Be our redeemer and protector.
   (Listen to the reading of the Word of God.)
2. Glory to God in the highest,
   and peace to his people on earth.
3. The Lord is near to all who call on him.
   He himself will come to save us.
   Come, Lord Jesus; come and save us.
   Show us the glory of God. Amen.

CHAPTER 13

Jesus Is the Light of the World

Make up a story to fit this picture.

- Where are Tom and Maryellen going?
- Why?
- Why did Tom bring his flashlight?
- Why didn't Tom or Maryellen want to go alone?

Jesus is our light.

He helps us see what to do.

He helps us see where we are going.

He helps us find what we are looking for.

Jesus is the light of the world.

When he saw Jesus, Simeon said,

"This child is the Savior you have promised, O God.

He is a light shining out for everyone."

from Luke 2.32

We Believe:

Jesus said, "I am the light of the world. No one who follows me will ever walk in darkness."

John 8.12

We Do:

We light three candles on the Advent wreath. We pray:

1. Come, Lord Jesus; come and save us.

   Show us the glory of God.

   Be our light that shines in the darkness.

   Be our redeemer and protector.

   (Listen to the reading of the Word of God.)

2. Send us your light and your truth.

   They shall lead us safely to your holy place.

3. The Lord is near to all who call on him.

   He himself will come to save us.

   Come, Lord Jesus; come and save us.

   Show us the glory of God. Amen.

CHAPTER 14

Jesus Says, 'Come, Follow Me'

A tiny bud opens slowly and becomes a beautiful flower.
Just so, Jesus grew slowly, guided by his parents.
He lived with his family in Nazareth,
studying, working, helping, praying,
and waiting for the time to begin his work.

From the root of Jesse a bud shall blossom.

from Isaiah 11.1

When Jesus was ready, he left
Nazareth. He went to many towns to
tell people about God. He loved the
people. He showed them how to love
one another. He wanted everyone to
live as he lived, to love as he loved,
to pray as he prayed.
He spoke to everyone who would
listen.
"Come, follow me," he said.

Do you follow Jesus?

We Believe:

Jesus calls to each of us, saying,
"Come, follow me."

We Do:

We light four candles on the Advent wreath. We pray:

1. Come, Lord Jesus; come and save us.

   Show us the glory of God.

   Be our light that shines in the darkness.

   Be our redeemer and protector.

   (Listen to the reading of the Word of God.)

2. Show me, O Lord, your ways.

   Teach me how to follow you, for you are God, my Savior.

3. The Lord is near to all who call on him.

   He himself will come to save us.

   Come, Lord Jesus; come and save us.

   Show us the glory of God. Amen.

Let's Look Back

A. What do people do during Advent to remember that Jesus came to save us? Why do people try to act more loving and kind at Christmas time?

B. Can you tell something about each of these words? You can look in the GLOSSARY on pages 131-133 for help.

Advent	Elizabeth	Savior
Bethlehem	Glory	Shepherd
Christmas	Magi	Zechariah

C. Do you remember these stories from the Bible? Tell one of these stories at home today.
- Mary and the Angel (Luke 1.26-38)
- Mary and Elizabeth (Luke 1.38-56)
- The Birth of Jesus (Luke 2.1-7)
- The Angels and Shepherds (Luke 2.8-18)
- The Wise Men and the Star (Matthew 2.1-12)

UNIT 4

Jesus Is Our Leader

CHAPTER 15

We Belong to God

John the Baptizer was the son of Elizabeth and Zechariah. John loved God. He wanted others to love God. "Change your way of living," he told them. "Do not be selfish. Turn your hearts to God."

Many people turned to God. John baptized them. "This baptism is a sign that you are sorry. It is a sign of your new way of living," he told them.

Jesus came to John. "Baptize me, too," he said. "I am beginning a new way of living. I am going to do the work my Father has given me." John baptized Jesus in the Jordan River. The Spirit of God was with Jesus. "You are my beloved Son," said God. "My favor rests on you."

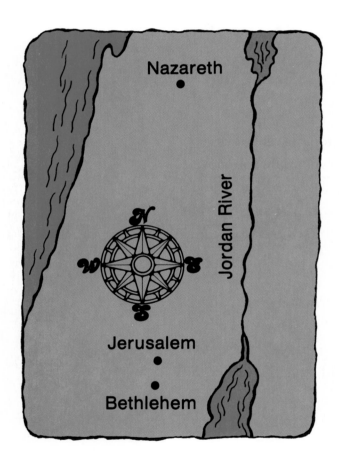

John told his friends to follow Jesus. "He is the Savior we have been waiting for," he said.

from Matthew 3

We Believe:

Baptism is the sign of a new way of living.

Baptism is the sign that we belong to God.

Baptism is the sign that we will follow Jesus.

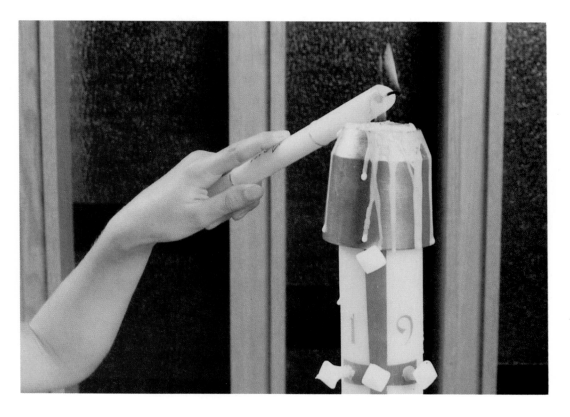

We Do:

Ask your parents about your baptism. Were you baptized in a river? Did you receive white clothing and a white candle? Do you have pictures?

We Belong to the Family of God

Beth and Amy Stith were very happy. Their new brother, Kevin, was coming home. They ran to the window when the car stopped in front of the house. Aunt Lynn, who was staying with them, threw open the front door. In walked Mr. and Mrs. Stith. In walked Kevin. "Oh, Beth!" said Amy. "Our new brother is not a baby!"

- Why was Amy so surprised?
- How did Kevin become Amy and Beth's brother?
- How will Beth and Amy and Mr. Stith and Mrs. Stith and Aunt Lynn show Kevin that he is part of their family?

What is the name of your family? How did you become part of that family?
How many ways can you think of to bring new members into a family?

Many people come on Sunday to pray together. They belong to many
families. But they are also part of one big family. They belong to the family of
God. They became part of that family when they were baptized.

Philip and the Traveler

Philip was very happy. He and the traveler had talked about Jesus. Now the traveler wanted Philip to baptize him. The traveler wanted to follow Jesus, too. He wanted to take the good news of God's love to his home in faraway Africa.
from Acts 8.27-39

- How is Philip's joy like the joy of Beth and Amy Stith?
- How will the Christian people show the traveler that he is part of their family?

64

We Believe:

Christians are baptized in the name of the Father, and of the Son, and of the Holy Spirit.

We Do:

Write a prayer telling God how happy you are to be baptized.

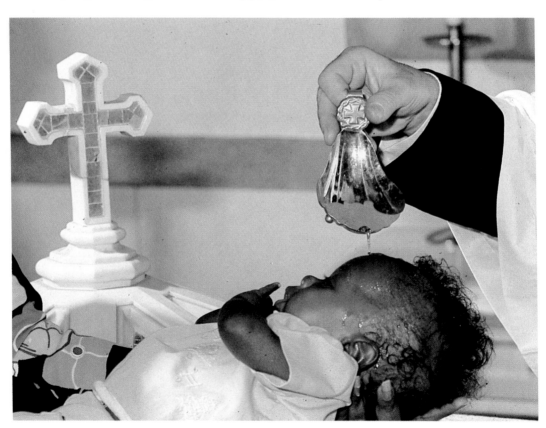

We Have Time to Grow

CHAPTER 17

Peter Pan did not want to grow up. He did not want to go to school. He did not want to wear a necktie or go to work. Peter Pan wanted to stay a child forever.

- Do you want to grow up?
- Are you growing now?
- How do you know?

A plant needs water to grow.
It needs sunshine.
It needs good soil.

We need help to grow, too.
We need food and water.
We need sunshine and exercise.
We need a home and lots of love.

People in families help each other grow.
How does your family help you grow?
How do you help your family grow?

The sacraments help us grow.

They help our whole Church grow.

Three sacraments are called SACRAMENTS OF INITIATION because they come at the *beginning* of our lives as Christians. (*Initiation* means *beginning.*)

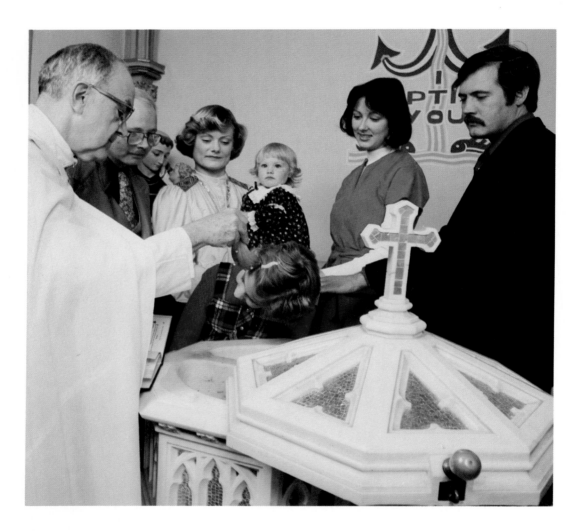

The three sacraments of initiation are:

BAPTISM — We begin to live as Christians.

CONFIRMATION — God makes our Christian life strong.

EUCHARIST — The life of Jesus feeds us.

The Church is a caring family.

How does the Church help you grow?

How do you help the Church grow?

We Believe:

Jesus said, "I have come that they might have life, and have it to the full."

John 10.10

We Do:

Do two things this week that will help someone grow.

- Can you make someone grow in happiness?
- Can you read someone a story?
- Can you help make your home peaceful?
- Can you teach someone a game?

Jesus Shows Us the Way

CHAPTER 18

Many sick people came to Jesus. Some could not see. Some could not speak clearly. Some could not walk. Jesus gave them his love. He cured them. These were gifts only Jesus could give.

Jesus told his followers, "If you have faith in me you will do the works I do."

from John 14.12

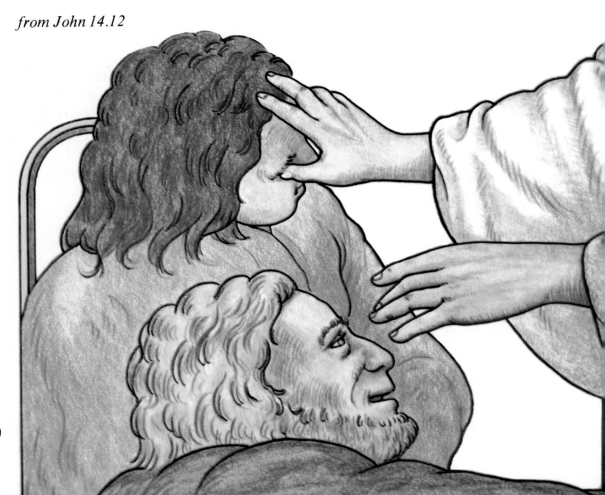

Many sick people came to Doctor Tom Dooley. Some were sick from hunger. Some were hurt in the war. Some had a disease. Tom Dooley tried to do what Jesus did. He gave the sick people his love. He cured many of them. These were gifts Doctor Tom Dooley could give.

Jesus wants us to help other people as much as we can. How can you help others now? How can you help others when you are older? What are the gifts that you can give?

We Believe:

Jesus helped people who needed help.

Jesus wants us to help, too.

Jesus said, "This is how everyone will know you are my followers. They will see how you love one another."

from John 13.35

We Do:

There are many people like Tom Dooley. Ask your family to tell you about someone else who loves Jesus and helps others. Tell the class what you learn.

CHAPTER 19

God's Love Is Forever

"Give me the cereal," said Sam.

"Get it yourself," said Greta.

Sam got the cereal box. He looked inside.

"It's all gone!" he said. "You took it all!"

"So what!" said Greta.

"So THIS!" said Sam. He poured orange juice on Greta's cereal.

- What should Greta do now?
- What should Sam do now?
- If you were Greta and Sam's parents, what would you do?
- Do things like this ever happen to you?

Jesus asks us to say "I am sorry" when we have been mean or selfish. Jesus asks us to forgive people who are mean to us.

Sometimes people sin. They decide not to live as Jesus asks. In their hearts they say to God, "No, I won't!" If we sin we can say "I am sorry" to God. God always forgives us because he loves us.

To teach us how much God loves us, Jesus told a story about a loving father.

The Story of the Loving Father

Once upon a time a boy asked his father for some money. Then he moved away from home. His father was very sad. The boy led a bad life. He wasted his money and hurt other people. He cared only for himself.

Soon he had spent all the money. He had nothing. He got a job caring for pigs. He ate what the pigs left. He was lonely and unhappy. Then he said, "I will go back to my father. I will work for him. I will tell him I'm sorry."

The father had been watching every day for his son. He worried about him. He loved him every minute of every day. When he saw his hungry, unhappy son coming down the road, he ran to meet him. Before the boy even could say, "I am sorry," the father hugged him and took him home.

from Luke 15.11-24

75

We Believe:

When we refuse to live as God asks us to live, we sin. God, our Father, always loves us. He will always forgive us.

We Do:

Have you ever acted in a mean or selfish way on purpose? If you can remember a mean or selfish thing you did, write a prayer telling God that you are sorry for these actions. Tell him that you will try to do better with his help.

Signs of Forgiveness

CHAPTER 20

Making Up

Lester sat on the blue chair. He looked at his shoes.

Lena sat on the green chair. She looked at her shoes.

They did not say anything.

"Well?" said Mother. "Who will begin?"

"I want to go and play," said Lester.

"Not until you and your sister are friends again," said Mother.

Lena did not want to say "I am sorry."

Lester did not want to say "I am sorry."

They did NOT want to hug each other! But Mother would not let them go until they made things right again.

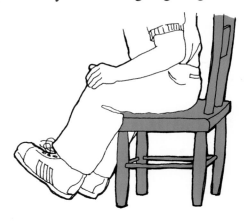
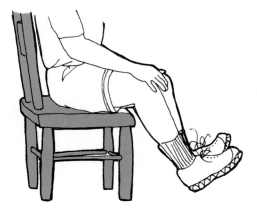

- Why do you think Mother made this rule?
- Do you think it is a good rule?
- Will Lester and Lena be happier when this is all over?
- How do you make things right again in your family?

The Church helps adults and children make things right again.

Here are five ways the Church helps us find forgiveness and peace.

1. We can talk to one of our older brothers or sisters in God's family.

2. With the priest, we can celebrate forgiveness in the sacrament of penance.

3. We can ask for God's forgiveness in the penitential rite of the Mass. (*Penitential* means *being sorry for what we did wrong.*)

4. We can show forgiveness and friendship in the peace rite of the Mass.

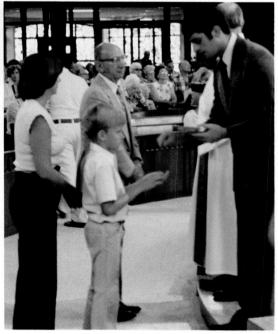

5. We can receive the Eucharist. **79**

Catholics celebrate God's forgiveness and peace in the SACRAMENT OF PENANCE.

- They greet the priest.
- They listen to God's Word.
- They tell their sins.
- They say they are sorry and will try to be good.
- They listen to the priest's prayer of forgiveness.
- They do a penance. (A *penance* is *an action that shows they are sorry.*)

This is also called the SACRAMENT OF RECONCILIATION. (*Reconciliation* means *making things right again.*)

We Believe:

The Bible tells us:

"If any of you have committed sins,
you will be forgiven.
Tell your sins to one another,
and pray for one another,
that you may find healing."

from James 5.15-16

We Do:

- Ask the adults in your home if they ever say "I am sorry" to each other.
- Ask them to tell you how they use the Church's five ways to forgiveness and peace.
- Try to do the penitential rite and the peace rite better next Sunday.

Let's Look Back

A. Those who follow Jesus are the Church. Can you tell about the things people of the Church do or believe? Tell one thing on each of your ten fingers.

B. Can you tell something about each of these words? You can look in the GLOSSARY on pages 131-133 for help.

Church	Penitential rite	Sacraments of initiation
John the Baptizer	Reconciliation	Sin
Peace rite		

C. Do you remember these stories? Which ones are from the Bible?
- The Baptism of Jesus (Matthew 3).
- Philip and the Traveler (Acts 8.27-39).
- Jesus Cures People (Matthew 15.29-31).
- Doctor Tom Dooley Cures People.
- Saint Elizabeth Seton.
- The Loving Father (Luke 15.11-24).

Celebration of Healing

Call to Prayer

Leader: We are members of God's family.
We should help each other.
We should forgive each other.
We should live as Jesus taught.
Sometimes we don't live that way.
Sometimes we are mean.
Sometimes we lie.
Sometimes we won't help others.
Our family, the Church, will help us.
Our family, the Church, will heal us.
Our family, the Church, will forgive us.
(Period of silence.)

Penitential Rite

Leader: For the times we have made others feel lonely or unhappy: Lord, have mercy.

All: Lord, have mercy.

Leader: For the times we have caused unhappiness at home: Christ, have mercy.

All: Christ, have mercy.

Leader: For the times we have not prayed for help to live as Jesus taught: Lord, have mercy.

All: Lord, have mercy.

Leader: If anyone would like to ask Jesus and us for help with some other failing, please feel free to ask now. (Pause.)

Leader: God, our Father, forgive us. Help us to be more like Jesus each day. We ask this in his name.

All: Amen.

Liturgy of the Word

Reader:	A reading from the gospel of Saint Matthew.
All:	Glory to you, Lord.
Reader:	Jesus was walking along a road. Two blind men followed him.
Blind Men:	Son of David, have pity on us. Please help us, Jesus.
Jesus:	Do you really believe that I can heal you?
First Blind Man:	Yes, Jesus, we know that you can heal us.
Second Blind Man:	We believe that you can do it, Jesus.
Reader:	Jesus touched the eyes of the blind men. He said. . .
Jesus:	Because you have faith in me, you will see.
First Blind Man:	Wow! I can see! I see trees and people and rocks!
Second Blind Man:	I can see, too! Look at the sun and the birds and the flowers!
Jesus:	I am glad to make you so happy. Don't tell anyone that I healed you. Let this be our secret.
Reader:	But the men were so happy they told everyone they met about Jesus.
First Blind Man:	Did you hear about Jesus? He is a good man who helps everyone. I am going to try to be just like him. Can I help you with anything?
Second Blind Man:	Jesus is so good that he doesn't want everyone to know the good things he does. He does good things out of love. He doesn't want praise. I want to be just like him.
Reader:	And Jesus looked at the many unhappy people whom he met and said. . .
Jesus:	Come to me, all of you who are worried and discouraged, and I will help you. Follow me. Learn from me. I am gentle and happy to be just myself. I

will heal you and help you every day.

from Matthew 9.27-31; 11.28-30

Reader:	This is the gospel of the Lord.
All:	Praise to you, Lord Jesus Christ.

Homily:

Discuss the reading with your teacher.

Leader:	Let's be quiet and tell Jesus about our problems. Then let's listen very hard as he tells us how to be better.
Leader:	As a sign of our friendship with one another, let's greet each other with the sign of peace just as we do at Mass.

All share the handshake of peace.

Sing a song of thanks and praise.

God Feeds His People

A Place
at the Table

CHAPTER 21

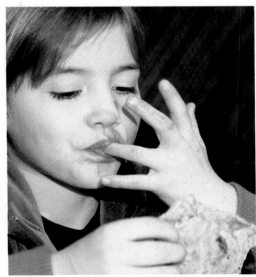

Eating is wonderful.
Being part of a family is
wonderful, too.
Eating with your family
is one of the nicest things
you can do.

People who eat together often get to know each other very well. They share their food. They share their stories. They share their lives.

Eating keeps us alive.
Sharing keeps us alive.
Loving people keep us alive.
The food we share is a sign of life.

The Eucharist is the family meal of the Church.
At the Eucharist Christians share their food.
They share their stories.
They share their lives.
At the Eucharist Christians receive the Bread and Wine that are Jesus.
Jesus gives his life to his family at their family meal.

We Believe:

Jesus said: "I am the bread of life. No one who comes to me shall ever be hungry, no one who believes in me shall ever thirst."

John 6.35

We Do:

During Lent the Church tries to put food on the tables of hungry people around the world. Find out what your family and parish are doing to help.

Special Days, Special Foods

CHAPTER 22

We gather to celebrate:

the number of days we have lived,

that our nation is free,

the beginning of a new family,

the good things God has given us.

We use food to help us
celebrate.

To have food we need God.

Food helps us celebrate God's goodness.

To have food we need people working together.

Food helps us celebrate each other's goodness.

Food is needed for life.

Food helps us celebrate the gift of life.

Food makes us feel welcome.

92
Food helps us celebrate the joy of being together.

Every Sunday the parish celebrates.
Food helps us celebrate.

Bread and wine are a gift from us.
It says, "You are our God; we thank you."

Bread and Wine are a gift to us. It says, "You are my people; I love you."   **93**

We Believe:

Bread and wine are the food of our Sunday celebration. They are blessed, or consecrated. They are the Body and Blood, the life and strength of Jesus.

We Do:

Mahatma Gandhi was a holy man. He prayed for his starving people. He said that "the only way God can visit hungry people is to come in the form of bread."

Ask your family what this saying means.

Tell the class why it is a good saying to remember during Lent.

We Remember God's Love

Every year the Klein family celebrates the feast of Passover. They eat a special meal to thank God for saving their people. The meal is called the Seder.

Rabbi Klein says:

- On this night we remember the good things God has done for us.
- On this night we thank God for the good things he is still doing for us.
- On this night we remember that we are God's chosen people.

All over the world our Jewish brothers and sisters celebrate the Seder at Passover. They did this in the time of Moses. They did this in the time of Jesus. They will do it this year, too.

At the Seder someone tells how God freed his people when they were prisoners, and fed them when they were hungry. The leader holds the Seder bread and says, "This is the sign of those sad days. We pray that next year everyone in the world will be free. Let all who are hungry come and eat. Let all who are in need share this Passover with us."

We Believe:

The Passover reminds us that God's saving love never ends.
God will not forget the people he has freed.
God will not forget the people he has fed.

We Do:

Let us pray with our Jewish brothers and sisters:

We thank you, Lord our God, for all the good things you have done for us. You have brought us from slavery to freedom, from sadness to joy. We will thank you from the time the sun rises in the morning until it sets in the evening. You, O God, are greater than the world you have made, and yet you care about each one of us.

We Remember Jesus

CHAPTER 24

Jesus loved his people. They loved him, too. They needed him. They wanted him to stay with them forever. "Yes," he said. "I will always be with you. When you remember what I have taught, when you remember what I have done, when you remember me —
I will be with you."

Jesus took bread. He gave thanks to his Father. He broke the bread and gave it to his friends. He said:

"Take this and eat it. This is my body which will be given up for you."

Jesus took the cup of wine. He gave thanks to his Father. He gave the cup to his friends and said:

"Take this and drink from it. This is the cup of my blood. It will be shed for you and for all, so that sins may be forgiven.

Do this in memory of me."

This happened at the last supper Jesus ate with his friends before he died and rose.

from Matthew 26.17-30 and Luke 22.7-20

After Jesus died and rose, his friends remembered the Last Supper. "Jesus is with us in this special meal," they said.

"It is a new Passover meal for us."

They called this holy meal the EUCHARIST.

Eucharist means *thanksgiving.*

This meal is also called the Mass.

We Believe:

When we celebrate the Eucharist, we remember the life, death, and resurrection of Jesus.

When we celebrate the Eucharist, Jesus is with us.

We Do:

At every Eucharist Catholics pray for people who need help.

Why is this prayer a good one to remember during Lent?

Leader: For people who are hungry, let us pray to the Lord.

All: Lord, have mercy, hear our prayer.

Leader: For people who don't have clothes, let us pray to the Lord.

All: Lord, have mercy, hear our prayer.

Leader: For people who don't have parents or friends, let us pray to the Lord.

All: Lord, have mercy, hear our prayer.

Leader: For people who are trying to help others during Lent, let us pray to the Lord.

All: Lord, have mercy, hear our prayer.

Leader: We ask this through Christ our Lord.

All: Amen.

Jesus Lives!

CHAPTER 25

When Jesus died, his friends were very sad.

"He is gone forever," they thought. But on the third day Jesus rose from the dead. He went to see his friends.

"Do not ever be sad again," Jesus said; "I will always be with you."

The Church remembers that Jesus is risen.
The Church remembers that Jesus is alive.
The Church celebrates this on Easter.
The Church sings ALLELUIA!

Christ has died.

Christ is risen.

Christ will come again.

This is the good news of the resurrection.

We Believe:

We will be raised from death through the power of Jesus.

We Do:

Jesus said that when we are raised from death he will say to us, "Come! You have my Father's blessing.

For I was hungry
    and you gave me food.
I was thirsty
    and you gave me drink.
I was a stranger
    and you took me in.
I was naked
    and you clothed me.
I was ill
    and you comforted me.
I was in prison
    and you came to visit me.
As often as you did it for the least of God's children you did it for me."

from Matthew 25.31-40.

Ask your family what this teaching means.

Let's Look Back

A. People usually mark special days with special foods. Can you think of times when special foods are important to you? Name one of those times on each of your ten fingers.

B. Can you tell something about each of these words? You can look in the GLOSSARY on pages 131-133 for help.

Alleluia	Eucharist	Mass
Consecrate	Last Supper	Passover
Easter	Lent	Resurrection

C. Do you remember these stories from the Bible? Tell one of these stories at home today.

- Jesus Feeds the Hungry People (John 6.1-14)
- Let My People Go (Exodus 5, 6, and 12)
- A Gift to Remember Me By (Matthew 26.17-30 and Luke 22.7-20)
- A Surprise on the Road to Emmaus (Luke 24. 13-35)

UNIT 6

We Give Thanks Through Jesus

We Come to Mass

CHAPTER 26

Aretha Jones gives her father a hug as he gets off work. Mr. Jones and the other workers make shoes in the factory. They make hundreds and hundreds of shoes. Mr. Jones could not do it alone. It is a work they must do together.

Can you think of other work that is too big for one person to do alone?

On Sunday the whole parish comes to celebrate the Eucharist. This celebration needs all the followers of Jesus in the parish.

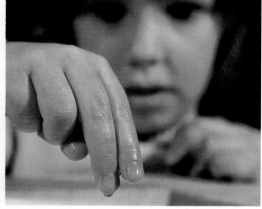

Water reminds us of baptism. We were baptized into one family. As one family we offer the Mass.

110 We sing praise and thanks with one voice.

Jesus said, "Be reconciled to your brothers and sisters before you bring gifts to my altar."

from Matthew 5.24

At the penitential rite we pray for people we have hurt. We tell God we are sorry to hurt any of his people. We forgive those who hurt us. We ask God to help us do better.

LORD, HAVE MERCY
CHRIST, HAVE MERCY
LORD, HAVE MERCY

We Believe:

The celebration of the Eucharist is the action of the entire Church. Each time we offer the Mass, Jesus acts with us.

We Do:

Jesus said, "When you start to pray, forgive anyone who has hurt you. Then your heavenly Father will forgive you, too."

from Mark 11.25

Each night, before you sleep, think about your day.
   Did anyone hurt you? Did they make you angry? Did they take your things?
Forgive them with all your heart.
   Did you hurt anyone? Were you mean? Did you disobey?
   Did you forget to say "I am sorry"?
Ask God to forgive you with all his heart. You can be sure that he will.

We Listen to God's Word

CHAPTER 27

The Bible tells about the great things God has done. It reminds us of his love and his care.

The Bible tells about Jesus. It reminds us that Jesus is our Savior and our Lord.

The Bible tells about the Spirit of God. It reminds us that the Holy Spirit guides the Church and helps us grow.

The Bible is God's gift to us. It is a sign of God's love.

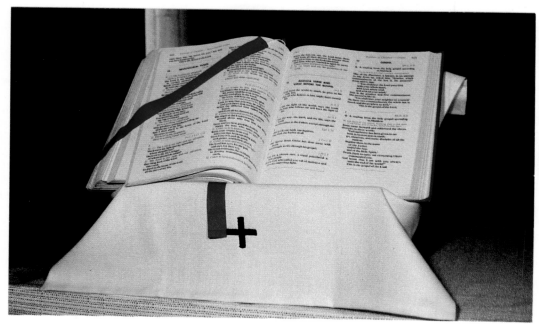

A reading from the holy gospel according to Matthew.
Glory to you, Lord.
"A farmer went out to plant his fields. As he went along, he scattered the seeds by hand. Some of the seeds blew onto the road, and were eaten by birds. Some of the seeds fell on rocks, and they could not grow. Some of the seeds fell where weeds and thorn bushes were growing. When they grew, they were killed by the weeds. But most fell on good, rich soil. They grew into a fine harvest."
from Matthew 13.4-23

This is the gospel of the Lord.
Praise to you, Lord Jesus Christ.

114

The readings at Mass are taken from the Bible. We listen to the Word of the Lord in order to live and grow.

God speaks to us as his children. God speaks to us as a community.

The priest knows that God's Word is a living word. His homily helps us think about what the readings mean.

We Believe:

Jesus is present when the Word of God is read to his people at Mass.

We Do:

- Tell a story from the Bible at home today.
- Ask someone at home to find this part of the Bible for you:
  The Gospel of John, chapter 11, verses 25 through 27.
  Read the words of Jesus that you see there.
  Draw a picture of what Jesus' promise means to you.
  Show it to the class.

We Give and Receive Gifts

CHAPTER 28

Give names to the people in this picture.

Tell a story about them.

- Who is giving the gift? Why?
- What will the other person say?
- How will the other person feel?
- How does the gift-giver feel?

There are three gifts in this picture. Can you find them?

One Leper Remembered

Jesus cured ten lepers. They were all happy. But only one came back to thank him. Only one leper gave Jesus a gift in return.

from Luke 17.11-19

How can we thank God for all he has given us? How can we remember the gift of Jesus? We can give gifts in return.

We give bread and wine.

We give our work.

We give our love.

We give ourselves.

At Mass we give the gift of praise and thanksgiving.

We sing, HOLY, HOLY, HOLY LORD,
          GOD OF POWER AND MIGHT.

At Mass, Jesus gives himself to his people. "This is my body. This is the cup of my blood."

We sing, CHRIST HAS DIED, CHRIST IS RISEN,
          CHRIST WILL COME AGAIN.

At Mass, we join with Jesus and his Holy Spirit. We give glory and honor to the Father.

We sing, AMEN!

We Believe:

At Mass we thank God by offering and consecrating bread and wine. These gifts stand for us. At Mass God gives us the gift of his Son, Jesus. This is the greatest gift of all.

We Do:

- Think of a gift of service you can do.
    Give that gift to someone this week.
- Think of a gift that you can make.
    Make it and give it to someone this week.
- Tell God, in prayer, about the gifts you gave.

We Receive
the Lord Jesus

CHAPTER 29

Many grains of wheat make one loaf of bread. Many followers of Jesus make one Church. The bread of the Eucharist is a sign that we are one Church.

Jesus prayed, "May they all be one, Father."

from John 17.21

We have one Father.

Our Father, who art in heaven, hallowed be thy name; thy kingdom come; thy will be done on earth as it is in heaven. Give us this day our daily bread; and forgive us our trespasses as we forgive those who trespass against us; and lead us not into temptation, but deliver us from evil. Amen.

We are one parish family.

The Lord's peace be with you.

We share in the one bread, one cup.

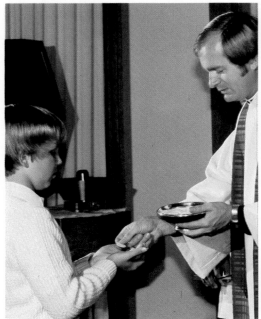 

The Body of Christ.

124 *Amen.*

The Blood of Christ.

Amen.

We Believe:

The Eucharist is the sacrament of unity. The Eucharist is the sacrament of love.

We Do:

When we receive Holy Communion the parish sings with joy. Then we are quiet, so that Jesus may speak to each heart. How will you answer Jesus?

Learn this prayer for communion time.
"Show me your ways, O Lord.
Teach me how to follow you,
for you are God, my Savior."

from Psalm 25.4-5

The Holy Spirit Leads Us

CHAPTER 30

The Mass ends. We are sent home.
We are sent to live and grow.
We are sent to help and share.
We are sent to love as Jesus loved.

Go in peace to love and serve the Lord.
Thanks be to God.

The parish sings with joy.

We took gifts to Mass.

We gave our thanks.

We gave our work.

We gave our hearts.

We bring a gift home with us.

God has given us his Son, Jesus.

God has given us his Holy Spirit to be with us.

Once the followers of Jesus were afraid. The Holy Spirit helped them. We can call on the Holy Spirit when we are afraid. The Holy Spirit is God's strength.

We can call on the Holy Spirit when we don't know what to do. The Holy Spirit is God's wisdom.

We can call on the Holy Spirit when we are lonely. The Holy Spirit is God's love.

We Believe:

God is our Father who loves us.
Jesus is our Savior and our Brother.
The Holy Spirit is our Helper and our Guide.

We Do:

The summer is a gift.
We will greet the summer with joy.
We will thank God for the summer.

We can say this prayer every day.
"Be happy, pray constantly,
and for all things give thanks to God,
because this is what God
expects you to do in Christ Jesus. Amen."

from 1 Thessalonians 5.16-18.

Let's Look Back

A. The Mass is a celebration of the Eucharist. It is a thanksgiving meal. It is a gift shared by Jesus and his people. It is a continuation of Jesus' sacrifice — his life, death, and resurrection. Can you name one of the things we do or say at Mass on each of your ten fingers?

B. Can you tell something about each of these words? You can look in the GLOSSARY on pages 131-133 for help.

Communion	Homily	Reading
Eucharist	Mass	Sacrament
Glory	Penitential rite	Sacrifice
Gospel	Priest	Thanksgiving
Holy Spirit		

C. Do you remember these stories? Which ones are from the Bible?
- One Leper Remembered (Luke 17.11-19)
- The Farmer and the Seed (Matthew 13.4-23)
- The Holy Spirit Comes to the Church (Acts 2.1-4)
- Saint Martin de Porres

Glossary

Advent — the time before Christmas when we open our hearts to Jesus.

Alleluia — (1) a word of joy; (2) used by people to praise and greet God, especially at Eastertime.

Anointing (of the Sick) — a sacrament; the priest anoints sick or dying persons and prays for them.

Baptism — a sacrament; our birth into the life of Jesus and his Church.

Bethlehem — town where Jesus was born; also the town where King David was born.

Bible — the written Word of God; the book that helps us know and love God better.

Catholic — a Christian who has been baptized into that church which has the pope as its leader.

Christian — one who follows Jesus and believes in his word.

Christmas — the day Christians celebrate the birth of Jesus.

Church — the People of God, who believe in him and work for his kingdom.

Communion (Holy Communion) — the meal part of the Mass; eating the Bread and Wine that are the Body and Blood of Jesus.

Confirmation — a sacrament; we receive strength from the Holy Spirit.

Consecrate — (1) to set something aside for religious use; (2) to bless the bread and wine at Mass changing it into the Body and Blood of Jesus.

Easter — the day we celebrate the resurrection of Jesus; most important holy day of Christians.

Elizabeth — mother of John the Baptizer; cousin of Mary.

Eucharist (Holy Eucharist) — a sacrament; the holy meal of Jesus and his Church; we renew the sacrifice of Jesus — his life, death, and resurrection.

Glory — praise, honor, worship, wonderfulness!

Gospel — (1) part of the Bible that tells about the life and work of Jesus; there are four of these; (2) a reading from one of the four gospels.

Holy Orders — a sacrament; a man becomes a deacon, priest, or bishop. **131**

Holy Spirit — God who is Love; God who is Strength; God who is Wisdom.

Homily — part of the Mass; the priest explains the readings.

Jesus — the Son of God and Savior of the world.

John the Baptizer — cousin of Jesus; a holy man who told people that Jesus was the Savior.

Joseph — (1) one of the holy men of the Bible; he forgave his brothers; (2) the husband of Mary; the foster father of Jesus.

Last Supper — the meal Jesus ate with his friends before he died; first celebration of the Eucharist.

Law of Love — the command Jesus gave his followers; it is on page 27.

Lent — the time before Easter when we prepare to celebrate the resurrection of Jesus.

Magi — wise men who came to see Jesus just after he was born.

Mary — the mother of Jesus.

Mass — the way Catholic Christians celebrate the Eucharist.

Matrimony (Marriage) — a sacrament; two people get married and become a new family.

Nazareth — the hometown of Mary and Joseph; the town where Jesus grew up.

Neighbor — whomever we know; whoever needs our help.

Parish — the group of Catholic families who live in one neighborhood and worship together.

Passover — the celebration to remember when God saved the Israelites from slavery in Egypt.

Peace rite — part of the Mass; we shake hands and wish each other the peace of Jesus.

Penance (Reconciliation) — a sacrament; we receive the forgiveness and peace of God.

Penitential rite — part of the Mass; we ask for forgiveness for what we have done wrong.

Priest — (1) an official who is chosen to teach about God and lead prayer; (2) a man who works with the bishop to guide the Catholic Church.

Reading — short part of the Bible that is read during the liturgy.

Reconciliation — making things right again; sacrament of reconciliation — see Penance.

Resurrection — Jesus was raised from the dead by the power of God; we share in his resurrection.

Sacrament — sign of the love of God and the faith of his people; sign of the life of Jesus in his Church.

Sacraments of initiation — Baptism, Confirmation, and Eucharist; the three sacraments that make us members of the Church.

Sacrifice — (1) the difficulty we sometimes experience when we help others; (2) the suffering and death that Jesus experienced when he became our Savior.

Savior — (1) any person who saves someone from danger; (2) Jesus, who saves us and gives us life.

Shepherd — (1) a person who takes care of sheep; (2) a person who cares about people and protects them.

Sin — a non-loving action that we do on purpose; living in a way that is not the way God has taught us to live.

Thanksgiving — (1) any time when we thank God for his gifts; (2) a day when Americans thank God for his goodness.

Zechariah — father of John the Baptizer; a Jewish priest.

Prayers

The Sign of the Cross

In the name of the Father, and of the Son, and of the Holy Spirit. Amen.

Hail Mary

Hail, Mary, full of grace! The Lord is with you. Blessed are you among women, and blessed is the fruit of your womb, Jesus. Holy Mary, Mother of God, pray for us sinners, now and at the hour of our death. Amen.

Glory Be to the Father

Glory be to the Father, and to the Son, and to the Holy Spirit. As it was in the beginning, is now, and ever shall be, world without end. Amen.

An Act of Contrition

My God, I am sorry for my sins with all my heart. In choosing to do wrong and failing to do good, I have sinned against you whom I should love above all things. I firmly intend, with your help, to do penance, to sin no more, and to avoid whatever leads me to sin. Our Savior Jesus Christ suffered and died for us. In his name, my God, have mercy.

(From the *Rite of Penance*)

Grace Before Meals

Bless us, O Lord, and these your gifts which we are about to receive from your bounty, through Christ our Lord. Amen.

Prayers of Thanksgiving (see pages 16 and 42). Celebration of Belonging (see page 21). Advent Wreath Prayers (see pages 47, 50, 53, and 56). Celebration of Healing (see page 83). Passover Prayer (see page 98). Prayer for People in Need (see page 103). The Lord's Prayer (see page 123). Prayer After Communion (see page 125). Prayer for Summer (see page 129).

Liturgical Responses

Lord, have mercy.
Christ, have mercy.
Lord, have mercy.

•

This is the word of the Lord.

Thanks be to God.

The Lord be with you.
And also with you.

•

Alleluia.

•

A reading from the holy gospel. . .
Glory to you, Lord.

•

This is the gospel of the Lord.
Praise to you, Lord Jesus Christ.

•

For _____ *(name)*, let us pray to the Lord.
Lord, hear our prayer.

•

Lift up your hearts.
We lift them up to the Lord.
Let us give thanks to the Lord our God.
It is right to give him thanks and praise.

•

Holy, holy, holy Lord,
God of power and might,
heaven and earth are full of your glory.
Hosanna in the highest.
Blessed is he who comes in the name of the Lord.
Hosanna in the highest.

•

Christ has died. Christ is risen. Christ will come again.

•

Through him, with him, in him, in the unity of the Holy Spirit, all glory and honor is yours, almighty Father, forever and ever.
Amen.

The peace of the Lord be with you always.
And also with you.

•

The Body of Christ.
Amen.
The Blood of Christ.
Amen.

•

Go in peace to love and serve the Lord.
Thanks be to God.

Things to Know

The Works of Mercy. See page 106.

The Law of Love. See page 27.

How to celebrate the sacrament of penance. See page 80.

How to receive Holy Communion.
  Receive the Sacred Bread in your hands.
    1. Put one hand on top of the other; hold them out like a bowl.
    2. The Sacred Bread is put in your hand.
    3. Answer, "Amen."
    4. Take the Sacred Bread with the other hand and eat it.
  Receive the Sacred Bread on your tongue.
    1. Answer, "Amen."
    2. Hold out your tongue; do not close your eyes.
    3. The Sacred Bread is put on your tongue.
    4. Take it into your mouth and eat it.
  Receive the cup of Sacred Wine.
    1. Answer, "Amen."
    2. Take the cup with both hands.
    3. Drink a little Sacred Wine.
    4. Return the cup.
  Some parishes have special customs. When you are in a new church, watch.
136 Do what others do. If you are not sure, ask about it.